To:

....

From:

....

A Warm Cup of Kindness is a trademark of West Side Publishing.

West Side Publishing is a division of Publications International, Ltd.

Louis Weber, CEO
Publications International, Ltd.
7373 North Cicero Avenue
Lincolnwood, Illinois 60712

ISBN-13: 978-1-4127-1579-9
ISBN-10: 1-4127-1579-2

Manufactured in China.

8 7 6 5 4 3 2 1

A Warm Cup of Kindness™ for MOTHER

WEST
SIDE
PUBLISHING

Contents

chocolate

A Mother's Love

There are only a few things in life we can always count on, and a mother's love is one of them. Like a steaming cup of tea on a cold winter day, or that favorite blanket you reach for when the air outside begins to feel crisp and cool, nothing quite compares to the one thing that feels like coming home—a mother's love.

The bond between a mother and child is unlike any other. It comes in all different shapes and sizes, colors and packages. There are moments when only a mother's love can do the trick, as well as moments that only in-the-trenches moms can recognize. *A Warm Cup of Kindness™ for MOTHER* is a collection of stories that captures these moments and the different packages in which you'll find them. Because, let's face it, whether it's your doting mother, or whether you're the doting mom yourself, no mother and no mother's experiences are ever exactly the same.

A mother knows when she's needed, and sometimes she even knows when to step back. She recognizes when you need her help through a breakup, and she knows when all you really want is a hug. Through those tough times that are bound to come, she's there when you need her.

Being a mother is also an experience unlike any other. Two o'clock-in-the-morning feedings, late nights with sick toddlers, early mornings making lunches, and washing load after endless load of clothes and towels can all make you feel like you're facing the challenges of motherhood alone. But here's the good news—whatever you're going through, and whatever struggles, uncertainties, or worries you have, there are millions of other women who have gone through the exact same things. And when you become a parent, you get automatic membership into the worldwide network of mothers, each of whom can identify with your hopes, your fears, and everything in between.

Whether you're the mother of a single newborn or the mother of teenage triplets, whether you have a gaggle of girls, a boatload of boys, or a handful of each, every mother shares an immediate bond—with each other and with their children. *A Warm Cup of Kindness™ for MOTHER* shares the hard-won insights and moments of glory—and humiliation—a mother goes through. And when the challenges of motherhood are testing  your patience, what could be better than sitting down for a piping mug of comfort and a few moments of chitchat and laughter from someone who's been in your shoes?

When you need a dose of sympathy from your own mom or a quick pick-me-up, these stories will touch your heart and bring a smile to your face.

So, turn off the phone, put up your feet, and pick up this book. Leaf through, read a few stories, and treat yourself to *A Warm Cup of Kindness™*.

The Storybook Quilt

After my baby shower, I plopped down in my new rocker in the nursery, which smelled of fresh paint. Around me, gifts frothed out of bags and boxes. My friends had given me nearly every item on my gift registry. The crib linens matched the pink curtains. The lamp and bookshelf went well with the princess theme—as did the tiny pink shoes and storybooks about little girls in tutus and princesses in glittery gowns.

The only odd gift was from the person who should have given me the best gift of all, my mother. I pulled what looked like a hodgepodge of scraps from a pink gift bag. Mom had smiled proudly when I opened it. When I hesitated, she whispered, "Quilt." I forced a smile, muttered "Thanks," and continued to open the other gifts.

The quilt was large for a crib. Its patchwork of uncoordinated colored squares reminded me of the Little Match Girl, who was so poor that she wrapped herself in rags to sell matches on a snowy street. My daughter would be a princess, not a pauper! What was Mother thinking?

I was chilly and tucked the quilt around my huge belly. I began to slide my finger along a blue velvet patch. The feel of the fabric brought back a memory of singing a solo at a recital when I was five years old. I remembered my stage fright, and how Mom had told me to take a deep breath for courage. In the end, I sang my heart out, and it felt so good. I noticed a square of green seersucker from my first day of school. I had torn my dress at recess, but Mom just hugged me harder and praised the "Good Job!" on my alphabet paper.

A dull brown patch had come from my Brownie uniform. Mom had been our troop leader. Also scattered on the quilt were the Girl Scout badges I had earned. Mom had been so patient with kitchen disasters as I worked my way through my cooking badge. A bit of pink flannel told the story of my first sleepover. A square of green satin spoke of being my cousin's junior bridesmaid. I snuggled deeper into the quilt, imagining sharing stories from my childhood with my daughter. I nodded off, wondering what other tales the quilt would tell me.

That night, instead of reading one of my three new parenting books, I was eager to "read" more of my quilt. But first I called my mother to thank her for the best gift of all.

Who Is Jane Schneider?

While writing thank-you notes to the people who had signed the guest book at our mother's funeral, my sister pointed to a name without a phone number or address. "Who is Jane Schneider?" she asked. I searched my memory but did not feel the slightest tingle of recognition.

"Do you remember meeting her at the funeral home?" my sister asked.

"No, but there were so many people. I didn't even know half of them."

Since we had both married and moved from New York to the West Coast, my sister and I couldn't expect to know all of our mother's friends. Still, we were so touched by the large turnout at her funeral that we wanted to thank everyone. Maybe after a good night's sleep, we would remember Jane Schneider.

The next morning, refreshed with orange juice, braced with coffee, and with bagels toasting in the oven, we sat at our mother's kitchen table and tried to solve the mystery from the night before. We went through her address book, leafed through her calendar, read her Christmas card list. No Jane Schneider.

"Maybe she's the scholarship girl from the inner city Mom sewed a college wardrobe for," my sister said.

"Or the woman with multiple sclerosis she took to the market every week," I suggested.

My sister nodded. "She could be the woman Mom wrote about in her Christmas letter, when she asked that we send money instead of presents so she could help a divorced mom get back on her feet."

"Remember the wives of foreign businessmen she taught how to shop, drive, and read?" I asked.

"Well, Jane isn't a foreign name, but didn't Mom say that some of them had such unpronounceable names that they used English ones?"

I sighed. "I guess Jane Schneider will just be one of Mom's little mysteries."

It wasn't until our second bagel that we realized Jane Schneider was many women. She represented all the women our mother quietly assisted. Our mother had such a generous nature that she never needed recognition or praise.

"I think we can best honor Mom's memory by finding a few Jane Schneiders of our own," my sister said.

And through the years, we have.

Mothers have the uncanny ability to know exactly what their children need, even when their children don't yet know it themselves.

Mother's Day Letter

"For Nick to read when he is grown," the envelope said. I have a tradition of writing letters to my kids at different times in their lives and saving them to read when they are older. This particular letter that I had written to my son, now 21, was dated Mother's Day, 15 years ago. He had been in kindergarten, and reading it brought back memories of the day I realized what a truly selfless, kind child I had been blessed with.

Dear Nicholas,

Today was Mother's Day. As I watch your beautiful sleeping face, I wanted to write this letter to give you later so you will always know how much joy you bring me.

You gave me the best present I've ever received today! It has a little story behind it that I will treasure forever. You have been diligently saving your allowance for weeks to buy some material for Grandma to use to make a tepee for you. You had $7 saved last week, but you asked me to take you to a nearby boutique where handmade crafts, which I love, were sold. You were so cute watching me as I looked at things, and if I liked something, you would ask how much it cost. We found an adorable little teddy bear with an antique-lace collar, a ribbon tied around its neck, and a ring attached. You pretended you loved it and even tried on the ring. You were very sneaky for

a five-year-old! You bought the bear all by yourself and said you were sorry because you spent all your money and would just make me something for Mother's Day. I would have loved anything you made!

This morning you woke me up with a big grin and a package wrapped in paper towels and tape. You were so proud and excited! Inside was the little bear that I will always treasure. You sacrificed your tepee for me.

I am so proud of your sweet, generous spirit and the many ways you bring me joy every single day. You are truly special, and I am honored to be your mother.

Love, Mom

I still have the bear and the little ring. And Nick did get his tepee that year for his birthday. I smile at the memories and place my letter for Nick in an envelope to mail to him, hoping that reading it will remind him what a miracle he is and how blessed I feel to be his mother.

Big Dipper Dreamin'

I won't do it this year, I thought to myself. I won't get myself worked into a tizzy all in the name of providing a memorable summer for my family. I'll keep the visions of beautiful picnic spreads under control and minimize the reunions and amusement park visits and everything else that leaves me gasping for air as I try to find the energy to shop for school supplies by Labor Day. This summer I vow to keep my planning to a minimum, and my family will end up happier for it. Of that, I'm quite sure.

One moment stands out as the prime example of having gone a tad too far with my need for perfection. It was late last August, school was about to start, and I couldn't help but reflect upon our whirlwind of a summer to make sure we had done everything I had set out to do. Boating weekends? Check. Amusement park? Check. Outings with cousins and grandmas? Check. Red, white, and blue buffets and ice cream cakes? Check. On paper it seemed that all of my efforts to create a perfect summer for my family were accomplished, but I had a gnawing, uneasy feeling. Did I take a deep breath and enjoy even a moment of it? Did I lie on the grass and watch the clouds float by? Did I check out the Big Dipper even one time? Nope.

This year I won't let that happen. I'm going to create a mantra to repeat should I start to forget. "I do not need to make star-shape finger sandwiches. I do not need to make star-shape finger sandwiches. I do not need to make star-shape finger sandwiches." Nor does anyone expect me to make lemonade from scratch or remove every telltale smudge of grass stain from my kids' clothing. After all, a good slide into third base needs proof, doesn't it?

As another chance at summer approaches, I'm forcing myself to reach for sidewalk chalk instead of my annual checklist. I'm going to let mushy peanut butter and jelly sandwiches replace pesto chicken. I'm going to let bedtime and bathtime fall by the wayside, and instead of watching my kids catch fireflies, I'm going to join them.

There is no way you can be a perfect mother,
but your children don't need perfection.
They need you, just as you are.

A Voice to Be Heard

At my mother's house one day, my four boys were breaking the sound barrier with trucks that added sirens and honks to the noise threshold I considered normal. I looked at my mother sitting across the kitchen table and realized that while my voice had been escalating, she had not said a word in 15 minutes. Amazingly, she did not look perturbed.

Embarrassed, I stomped into the family room and yelled, "Quit the yelling. Now!" I rejoined my mother at the kitchen table, and we resumed making plans for my sister Jenny's baby shower. Soon, the noise reached former levels, and I was shouting across the table again. My mother stopped talking and squeezed lemon in her tea. Still, she did not look annoyed. I attributed her patience to her years of teaching first grade.

I told her I would put a stop to the noise.

She put her hand on my arm and said, "My turn."

In the family room, the sudden quiet was like the eye of a hurricane. "Would you like cookies?" she asked. Her voice was so soft I had to strain to hear her.

With huge smiles, the boys nodded and gathered around her as she cut four chocolate chip cookies in half. She gave each one half of a cookie.

Their eyes held silent questions, waiting for her to speak.

"You can have the other half," she said, "after you play quietly for an hour." She continued, "See, I'm setting the timer. When it goes off, you can have the rest—but I won't be able to hear the timer if you're noisy."

In the unfamiliar atmosphere of children playing quietly, I asked her how she managed to survive both motherhood and teaching without ruining her vocal cords.

"I've been waiting for you to ask," she said. "As you know, I do not give my grown-up children unsolicited advice."

I nodded, acknowledging how grateful I am for her lack of interference.

"It was my first term of teaching first grade. When they got noisy, I increased my volume. They just got louder, and I ended up frustrated and hoarse."

"Been there," I said.

"I asked an experienced teacher, and she said, 'If you talk softly, children have to listen closely. So closely that they fall silent.'"

"And the cookies?"

"Stories! I'd read half a story first thing in the morning and promise to finish the story at the end of the day—but only if they behaved."

"So, you won't tell Jenny the secret until she asks, will you?"

"No, dear," she replied. "That's your job."

Becoming a mother means learning new things about yourself. How much sleep you can do without. How much patience you have. The best hiding place for chocolate.

Forget What the Experts Say

Every time I see a new study by a parenting "expert" I have to laugh. I'm sure these people are properly credentialed and have done their best to discover something that will be of help to parents. But I believe that the real reason they're researching the effect of salt on infants' sleeping habits and which wall colors enhance your child's intelligence is because even they are looking for answers. That's right—even these venerable professors, scientists, and doctors are clueless when it comes to what makes a good parent and a happy baby.

When I had my first child almost a decade ago, I was a dedicated, by-the-book parent. I read everything about pregnancy and childbirth that I could get my hands on. I swore off caffeine, choked down my prenatal vitamins, and aspired to be the perfect new mom. But as time passed, I realized that my son bore about as much resemblance to the babies described in the parenting manuals as my post-pregnancy body did to Angelina Jolie's. And the real questions I needed answers to—When will I feel like myself again? When will he sleep through the night? How can I get a shower in when he screams every time I set him down?—weren't in the books at all.

As my son grew, so did my confidence. Now that I'm the proud mom of three, I rarely pick up a parenting manual or read a how-to article. I've learned through trial and error how to make sure my toddler gets enough vitamin C (with all-fruit popsicles), and it was pure chance that led me to the solution for morning clothing battles with my middle child (choose a school with uniforms!).

My attempts to keep my family healthy, happy, and safe may make the "experts" cringe. Because, let's be honest, you won't find popcorn for dinner in the pages of any parenting book. The things that work for us aren't the same things that work for any other family on the face of the planet. The only way to really learn what works for you is to try a little bit of this and a little bit of that. And then if you want to see what kind of job you're doing, turn to the real experts—your kids. Are they clean? Healthy? Reasonably happy? Then you get an A+ in my book.

The Smells of Comfort

Regina drove down the long tree-lined dirt road that led to her mom's farmhouse. Growing up on a farm had been fun as a child, boring as a teenager, and insufferable as a young woman aching to see and experience the big world outside the boundaries of her rural Indiana town.

Life in the big city of Indianapolis was much more exciting, and Regina wasted no time landing a great job at a trendy interior design firm. She even met a great guy to go with the job. But every now and then, the comforts of her mom's warm house called her back for short and sweet visits.

Ten years had passed since she moved away. Now with a painful breakup and the rotten news that her company was bankrupt and she was out of a cushy job, Regina could think of nothing she wanted more than to find some solace and comfort in her childhood home with her loving, doting mom. As she turned into the gravel driveway to the house, she could smell the fresh scent of newly cut grass and the earthy sweetness of hay stacked against a weathered white picket fence.

Once she neared the sprawling white and yellow farmhouse, Regina felt her entire body relax as the odors of home greeted her. Freshly baked bread wafted from an open kitchen window, where she could see her mom bustling about. As she walked toward the door, she noted the unmistakable scent of apple pie, and it sent her back to the joys of childhood in a delightful flash. She had a vision of baking with her mother, wiping flour from each other's foreheads and laughing at the mess they were making in the cozy kitchen

Now Regina's life felt like a mess, and all she wanted was to see her mom. She didn't have to knock. Her mom opened the door and grabbed Regina into a warm embrace. Regina closed her eyes and let her mom hold her, feeling like a little girl again in need of comfort, breathing in the smells of flour and sugar in her mother's hair. In that moment, she knew everything would be all right. She was home again, with the one person who could make all the bad go away with nothing more than a hug and a piece of pie.

Dirty Little Reminders

I had been feeling something ugly brewing for days—probably weeks if I'm being honest. And by ugly, I don't mean the gray sunken circles under my eyes. Unfortunately, those are a given at this point. This particular kind of ugliness starts in the pit of your stomach and ends up as a worried furrow on your brow, exposing every forehead wrinkle you've ever had. As I hurriedly pulled the not-so-clean sheets over my bed and mentally went over all the things I unrealistically hoped to accomplish that day, the ugliness spewed out into a sentence that alarmed me—and finally brought some clarity.

"I'm just too involved with my family."

I stopped tugging at the sheets and realized the absurdity of that particular combination of words. "Too involved." "With family." Always one to be thrilled with creating an oxymoron, this one just seemed sad to me. Is helping my children get ready for their first day of elementary school too involved? Is coaching my daughter's first cheerleading squad and doing a nightly load

of grass-stained laundry from my son's football practice too involved? Is finally living up to the promise of a walk with the world's most patient black Labrador too involved? To top it all off, my husband doesn't even ask for any of my time at this point. He recognizes the bunched-up forehead and is steering clear.

That's when I heard it. The "ding, ding, ding" of the danger bells that always seem to peel at just the right moment, before I go over the edge and lose all sense of priority. In fact, at the very moment that I realized how much more important it is for me to nurture this beloved family of mine than to accomplish everything on my to-do list, I actually smiled. I smiled smack in the middle of a bedroom that needed to be dusted.

Suddenly, I felt better than I had in weeks. One simple sentence that raced through my brain had freed me, for the time being, from the myriad of tasks that were plaguing my brain. Taking my kids for haircuts and new sneakers aren't tasks, they're privileges. Laundry and emptying the dishwasher are tasks.

Sometimes we all just need a little reminder of the difference.

Surprise Me!

It had become a ritual. Every year when Christmas or her birthday rolled around, Krissa's mother asked her for some gift ideas. Because her mother was such an imaginative and thoughtful gift giver, Krissa always answered, "You know my taste. Besides, the best presents of all are the ones I would never have thought to ask for."

"Are you sure, honey? I want you to be pleased, not surprised," her mother would protest.

"Surprise me!" Krissa always insisted.

One year it was a cookbook, handmade with favorite family recipes and little stories about the aunts and grandmothers from whom the recipes had come, as well as a photo of Krissa wearing her mother's apron and baking cookies in the kitchen as a little girl. One year it was a vase Krissa had admired but couldn't afford the summer before when they were shopping. Her mother went back the next day and bought the vase, hiding it in the closet until Christmas. One year it was a coffee-table book with beautiful photographs of Italy, where their family had come from generations ago. Krissa had always wanted to go there with her mother. Inside the front cover of the book was Krissa's airline ticket.

When Krissa's mother became ill before they were to leave on their trip, Krissa tried to find just the right items to make her mother feel better—soaps in her favorite scent for her bath, a DVD of her favorite romantic comedy.

Krissa always assured her mother that before long, they would be going to Italy together. But one day there were dark circles under her mother's beautiful eyes, and she beckoned Krissa to climb up beside her on the hospital bed. She told her gently that while she wouldn't be going to Italy, she wanted Krissa to go with a friend instead and have a wonderful time. Through her tears, Krissa asked about her mother's last wishes. With the impish grin that Krissa knew too well, she said, "Surprise me!"

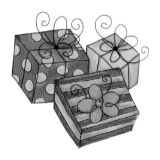

Setting for 12

Choosing a china pattern with my fiancé all those years ago wasn't quite the love fest a young girl dreams about all her life, but it *has* led to something quite lovely. There were a few things I quickly became aware of that summer evening in Marshall Field's. One was that the rolling of my betrothed's eyes meant that such decisions were to be mine from that point forward. The second thing I realized was that this particular decision was far more than just one of color or brand or pattern. It was the beginning of a tradition.

Once I fell in love with my Wedgwood china, I knew I had to do more than just serve Thanksgiving dinner on it. I felt an overwhelming desire to let these delicate serving pieces tell the tale of our new family to the next generation.

Just four weeks after my wedding, Thanksgiving was in the air. I was so excited for my mother and stepfather to share the meal with us. I shopped and chopped, cooked and baked, and finally it was time to work on my favorite thing—setting the table. Later, after belts had been loosened and the kitchen had been cleared, I sat in the empty dining room and recorded the day in my china journal, the notebook in which I recorded the experiences and adventures of my wedding china.

Twelve years and too many meals to count later, I'm still doing it. It's not the last chore of the day—far from it, actually. I imagine one day my daughter and her children leafing through the pages and feeling connected to the past, and dare I hope, to me. I imagine her laughing as she reads my menu and discovers that we both make deviled eggs for most holidays. She'll probably chafe when she reads that for the first few years I didn't grace her or her brother's place at the table with the Wedgwood china but with Barney plastic instead.

I hope that both my kids, as adults, read through the pages and see how many people we were blessed to have in our home throughout the years.

I realize that I'm putting a big burden on something as frail as porcelain. For I'm asking it to reflect love and tradition for years to come, long after I'm no longer here to represent it myself.

Making Up over Makeup

Days after the argument with my mother about how I was the only one in the entire senior class not allowed to go to Megan's party, I stomped home from school filled with nothing but self-righteousness. I had even given her the silent treatment for three days to no avail.

As I arrived home, her car was in the driveway. She did not greet me at the door with a hug and the usual questions: "How was your day? Do you need help with your homework?"

Was she ill? My rage evaporated as I ran to her room. Her door was shut. I knocked, but she didn't respond. I slowly turned the knob and walked in. She was sitting at her vanity with her head in her hands. Had someone died?

I hugged her, and she slowly raised her face. Something was odd about her eyes. It took me a few seconds to realize what was wrong. Her eyelashes and eyebrows were gone!

"Mom?" I said softly. Had she lost her mind?

"Your father is going to have a fit!" she exclaimed.

"He'll get you the help you need," I said, surprised by the adult tone in my voice.

"Erin, I don't keep much from your father, but this is one thing he can't find out about!" Her voice was strained as she explained how the furnace had gone out. Instead of illuminating that dim corner of the basement with a flashlight to relight the furnace, she struck a match. "The explosion blew me across the basement and, well, you can see what happened . . ."

"At least you still have your hair!" I said. Then I thought for a minute. "Remember the false eyelashes you wouldn't let me wear?"

She nodded.

"I didn't throw them away."

Relief washed over her face as I continued.

"And between us, we have enough eyebrow pencils to take care of those . . ."

She hugged me hard. We applied our combined beauty skills and supplies as best we could. She still looked a bit different, but we doubted my father would even notice the difference.

During dinner, he looked quizzically at Mom. "Your eyelashes look different," he said. "Have you been using Erin's makeup?"

"I forgot the gravy!" she cried, without skipping a beat, tipping over her chair in her flight to the kitchen.

I burst in right behind her, our shoulders heaving with suppressed laughter while my father called from the other room. "Girls? Girls! The gravy is on the table!"

A What Dress?

When my mother died, her sister promised her that she would be a mother to me. My aunt, Southern to the core, seldom visited because she lived in Alabama and I lived in Chicago. One day a birthday gift arrived, expertly sewn on her machine, that had me scratching my head. It was a dress patterned in pretty pastel flowers. It did not have zippers, buttons, or a belt. I reluctantly pulled it over my head and stared in the mirror. "Definitely not a nightgown and absolutely not my style," I thought. "At least not a style any woman I know would wear for any occasion that I could imagine."

I called my aunt and thanked her for the—I was hoping I had the right noun—dress. I said it was exactly what I needed. But I could not ask her what I needed it for. She replied, "Every woman needs a fresh doorbell dress, and it's not what you think to buy when you're out shopping."

"I just love my *doorbell dress*!" I made sure to emphasize my two new vocabulary words. A Google search returned no answers, so I hung the dress in my closet. Occasionally, I found myself asking a friend or colleague, "What's a doorbell dress?" I gathered an impressive collection of perplexed looks, but no answers.

Several years later at a national conference, I heard a Southern drawl. I immediately thought of my doorbell dress. Maybe she could enlighten me. I walked toward the woman and blurted out my question.

"Why, sweetie, don't you know?" Her eyes widened with surprise.

I confessed my ignorance as well as the ignorance of every woman north of the Mason-Dixon Line.

She explained. "When the doorbell rings and you're in your grubbies— changing the baby or scrubbing the floor—before you open the door you just slip on the pretty, fresh dress hanging beside it."

My door-opening debuts immediately flashed before my eyes—tugging down my son's football jersey to cover my thighs; wrapping a throw rug around my nightgown; my dripping, towel-wrapped body hiding behind the door; my baby-and-vomit look; my finger-painting phase; my covered-in-spaghetti-sauce conversation with a new neighbor.

After the conference, I rescued the mystery dress from a seldom-visited corner of my closet and hung it beside the door. I realized then that nothing could be smarter or do more for my pride than a doorbell dress! And I wouldn't have learned this trick without my Southern aunt, my surrogate mother.

My greatest moments of peace as a mother come amid the craziness of everyday life. When I hear my children laughing, playing, and even fighting, I know all is well. It's when everything is quiet that I start to worry!

One Fun Mom

Before I had children, I wanted to be the perfect mom. I wanted to be the one who had whole-grain, fresh-baked cookies waiting on the counter when the kids came in from school. The one who laid out clean, pressed, coordinated outfits to wear to church each Sunday. The one who always had a handkerchief, a safety pin, and a pack of baby carrots in her voluminous diaper bag.

Then I had kids, and my aspirations flew out the window along with my size-4 clothes and free time. The reality of the situation is that perfection isn't just overrated. It's impossible! Every mom comes to this realization and then must readjust her expectations accordingly. You can't be the home-baked cookies mom and the drives-on-all-field-trips mom. You can't be the hike-the-Grand-Canyon mom and the fashion-plate-and-clean-clothes mom. It just doesn't work that way. You have to choose.

So when I realized I couldn't have it all, I knew I had to make some tough decisions. How would my kids remember me decades from now? What would be my legacy? And then I chose. I wanted to be the fun mom.

I would be jump-on-the-bed mom, dance-in-the-kitchen mom, stay-up-late-and-go-to-Denny's-for-pancakes mom. Forget the pristine home and the educational trips to the children's museum. At our house we're having a sleepover in Mom and Dad's bed and reading ghost stories by flashlight.

Sure, sometimes I regret my choices, like when my daughter shows up at church wearing a pair of her brother's old jeans and a T-shirt. But for the most part, I'm giving my kids the childhood I want them to have—the one I wish I'd had myself. I lived a life of worry and angst and don't remember too many times of pure joy and goofiness. I want my kids to have something different, something better.

Not everyone will agree with my choice, and that's okay. In fact, it's great. Let's rejoice in our differences and use them to our advantage. I make deals with the other mothers now. If you take my kids to see the Renoir exhibit at the art museum, you can drop your kids off at my place for the evening. We're going on a bear hunt in the backyard.

Herstory

Three weeks after her mom passed away, Shawna found a large box tucked in the back of her mom's closet. She and her brother, Joe, had been cleaning out their mom's house, sorting through what they would keep and what they would toss.

Shawna felt a fresh pang of grief and loss for the mom she had thought of as perfect. Her mother, Ava, had been one of those stay-at-home moms, straight out of the 1950s, completely devoted to her family, especially her two children. Shawna imagined how boring her mom's life must have been and vowed she would live a more exciting life if she ever married and had kids.

She opened the box and was surprised to find bundles of old newspaper articles, letters, and several bound diaries. She unwrapped one of the bundles and sorted through the articles. She was shocked to see her mom, a much younger Ava, in a photo next to a headline that read "Anti-war activists arrested at Kent State." Shawna read the article, her mouth hanging open as she realized how her own mother spent two days in jail for taking part in a protest.

"I don't believe this," Shawna whispered as she began reading other articles. One showed Ava standing beside Tom Hayden and Jane Fonda at a civil rights rally. Another showed her near Martin Luther King, Jr.! Shaking her head in disbelief, she read through one of the letters. It was a passionate love letter to her mother from a man named Leo. Shawna's dad was named Frank, and as she read other letters, Shawna realized that before her mom was married, she'd had some passionate love affairs.

Shawna took out one of the diaries with a key attached and lovingly caressed the cover. She wanted to respect her mother's privacy, but she longed to know who this special woman, devoted to family in her later years, had been as a younger woman.

As she read on, she realized her mother was not boring, or bored, at all. She was an amazing woman, actively and passionately engaged in the world, who lived a full and exciting life and continued that legacy with the family she raised.

Inked

Liv cried as she looked at the calendar. Her divorce to Robert was final. Over. Done. Even though their marriage had emotionally ended years ago, it was still hard to deal with. She knew there would be a lot of firsts coming up, and that each one would be painful, but it would get better and easier over time.

The phone rang, and she didn't want to answer it, but it was her mom, Jo. Liv knew this was a hard day for her, too. Jo was turning the big 6–0 today and had asked that her family not throw a party. Liv answered, and sure enough, her mom was feeling just as down in the dumps as she was.

It felt strange. All her life Liv had counted on her mom for love, support, and courage when she had to go through challenges. Throughout the divorce, Jo had taken good care of her daughter, endlessly listening to Liv's tearful tirades and worries about being an old maid and never finding love again.

Now it was Liv's turn to listen, give back, and set aside her own emotional baggage to help her mom see that life didn't have to end at 60, and that with each ending came a new beginning. Jo suddenly smiled and said that what they needed was some special way to mark their new perspective on life.

Two hours later, Liv and Jo sat in a local tattoo parlor, cringing and giggling as they each got matching tattoos on their ankles. The image they chose was of a blooming rose to signify how their lives were about to bloom. Jo went first, crying from the pain, but feeling cleansed and excited, and even a little bit daring. When it was Liv's turn, Jo held her hand and talked her daughter through it, telling her funny stories about her childhood to keep her mind off the pain.

When it was over, they got their instructions for taking care of their new ink and left together giggling like schoolgirls. Jo stopped Liv outside and hugged her warmly, thanking her for reminding her that it's not over until she says it is. Liv thanked her mom for reminding her that life doesn't end after divorce, it just changes, and that sometimes change can be like a blooming rose, full of color, sweetness, and possibility.

Blooming Through the Generations

One autumn day when I was four years old, I squatted beside my mother, who was gathering seeds from the four o'clock plant beside our house. She put a few seeds in my hand and said they would bloom in the spring. As each season unfolded, I learned more about my family history through the presence of this special flower.

I learned that the original four o'clocks bloomed beside my great-great-great-grandmother's log cabin in the wilds of Wisconsin. I learned that even though my family moved from state to state and changed homes a half dozen times as I was growing up, the four o'clock flowers bloomed each and every spring beside the backdoor. Sometimes the flowers opened at five o'clock or even six. Either way, I was connected to generations of women from the time I could toddle by this humble, hearty species of flower.

The origin of the ancestral plant is lost in the mists of family lore, but through the generations, women in my family have passed down the seeds and planted them every spring. On my wedding day, my mother gave me an envelope. It was small and plain, but inside were the seeds that would bloom every spring of my life no matter where I lived.

They bloomed in a window box in Manhattan. They bloomed in several suburban backyards. Now they bloom beside the backdoor of my condo. When my daughter married, I gave her a small, plain envelope of four o'clock seeds. I was uncertain that customs would permit the transfer of four o'clock seeds to Korea, but today a four o'clock plant blooms in Seoul, where my daughter teaches.

Looking at the blossoms that open faithfully each day at four o'clock—or five or six—I wonder if my great-great-great-grandmother ever stood beside the door of her log cabin wondering about her daughters and their daughters. I know she could not have envisioned jet travel and computers. I know my granddaughters and great-granddaughters will live in a world I cannot imagine, but I have a sense that one thing will never change no matter how the world changes—four o'clocks will bloom in window boxes and backyards, reminding women of their roots and a strong pioneer woman who loved a humble, hearty species of flower.

Bridging the Gap

When I had my first child, people warned me that it would be difficult, if not impossible, to remain close to my friends who didn't have kids. "Once you cross that line, there's no bridging the gap!" they warned me. "You'll be thinking diapers and preschool while they're heading off to Bermuda and seeing every movie on opening weekend!"

But as my son got older, and as one baby became three, I discovered that keeping up with these child-less women was a piece of cake compared to trying to be close with others whose parenting styles are the antithesis of my own. There's the organic mom whose little treasure has never even seen refined sugar, let alone had a gummy bear cross his pristine lips. There's the Pottery Barn mom whose house looks like a spread from an interior design magazine—and whose kids aren't allowed to wear shoes in the house and must submit to an inspection with a lint roller before they are granted access to the living room. There's also the hypochondriac mom who won't let her child come within 20 yards of anyone who has had a sniffle in the past six weeks.

I don't want to disparage other parenting styles—after all, I've got my own foibles and quirks—but I do want to admit that it is a struggle to make these relationships work, even if a compatibility test would give us a score higher than that of Courteney Cox and Jennifer Aniston. But if the friendship is worth it, I've found ways to adjust.

I smartened up and started planning events *without* (gasp!) the kids, where moms could forget they were moms and concentrate on each other. I looked past the perfect family room and found the woman underneath, the person I could relate to and enjoy. And I learned to let my own parenting rules bend a little when the occasion called for it.

Why do I go to all this effort? Because I figure we're only parents part of the time. There will come a day when that *House Beautiful* is quiet, the cookie jar is empty, and the last temperature has been taken. And then we're not going to care who's tracking mud in the house or when their last tetanus shot was. We're going to need our friends.

Who Is Your Real Mother?

When Tamara was ten years old, her mother sat down beside her on the sofa and told her gently, but with a tone in her voice that she had never heard before, that she had something she needed to tell her. "You are adopted," she said. "Daddy and I couldn't have any children, and that broke my heart because I wanted so much to be a mother. Then we learned about a young woman who was going to have a baby but was not going to be able to take care of it. That young woman already loved the baby that she was going to have so much that she decided to give her to us, because she knew we would love the baby and take good care of it, just like she would have if she could."

Tamara felt tears come to her eyes. She choked them back and asked her mother, "Then you aren't my real mother?"

Her mother became a little teary, too. "I am your real mother because I raised you and loved you and took care of you the best I could. But the young woman who gave you life also took care of you the best she could, so she is your real mother, too."

Tamara still didn't see how she could have two mothers, and it troubled her. When she was 18, she wanted to meet her biological mother, but was afraid that this would hurt her mom. Her mom seemed to understand, however, and urged her to get in touch. Tamara's biological mother, who had gone on to marry and raise children of her own, was overjoyed to hear from Tamara. They stayed in touch, and it was with Tamara's adoptive mother's blessing that she invited her biological mother to come to her wedding.

Both mothers stood proudly alongside Tamara in the reception line. Afterward, a friend who had never met Tamara's parents and had been confused by the introductions asked her privately who her real mother was. "They both are," Tamara replied.

I am my mother's child.
You can see it in our smiles.

A Gift from the Past

My grandmother was a professor of English literature. Some considered this an academic step up from her mother, a high school English teacher. My mother taught freshman composition at a junior college while working on her doctorate. My grandmother often expressed how proud she was of all the teachers in our family—all the way back to my great-grandmother. Everyone assumed I would follow in the family footsteps; the only unknown was my academic focus. History or science would have been a new field, but literature would have been the traditional choice. All were worthy as long as they led to the teaching certificate. My grandmother would hang a copy of my certificate in her study along with her certificate, her mother's, and my mother's. We called it her trophy wall.

In college, I chose education as my focus, but the thought of facing a classroom did not inspire me. By the time I was a junior, I had developed a passion for journalism. But I did not want to teach it, I wanted to do it.

My mother was not surprised by this. She had recognized my talent in the school newspaper I edited and had read my passion for reporting between the lines of my articles. She said she was proud of me, and we would break the news to my grandmother together.

Sitting in her book-lined study, beneath her trophy wall, my grandmother poured tea and probed me about my studies. She pointed to the empty frame and noted that in a year, her wall would document four generations of female teachers. She pushed her glasses farther up the bridge of her nose and smiled proudly. Finally, I found the courage to tell her. She did not say anything, just focused her attention on an edition of my newspaper.

Abruptly, my grandmother left the room. When she returned, her skirt was dusty, and a wispy cobweb hung from her hair. She handed me a leather-bound journal that smelled of mothballs. The leather was cracked, the pages were yellowed. "This is your great-great-grandmother's," she said. "She would have been an accomplished journalist, but she had eight children and a homestead to run."

I looked at the empty frame, still uncertain of her feelings. She smiled and said, "That's for your first prize-winning article. Don't make me wait too long." She handed the journal to me. "I've been wondering for years which granddaughter I would give this to."

The Creation of Sunshine

"Cara, take off your rose-colored glasses!" My mom wasn't trying to be mean, I'm sure. But I've often thought back on that exact moment, and I think it was pure frustration on her part. She was a divorced young mother of three little girls, and every time she needed a sympathetic ear all she ever seemed to get from me was never-ending optimism.

Things weren't pretty back then—even I realized that. My father had remarried and finally squired the son he'd always wanted. My older sister was rebelling. Mom was working as a waitress while we were at school, and she seemed to scrub the ever-loving life out of every inch of our little ranch house in the evenings. The television broke. The washing machine broke. Mother Nature dumped a blizzard on Northwest Ohio, and it seemed that all 16 inches of that snow landed right in the middle of our driveway.

And then we found out just how bad things could really get. Mom's chest pains turned out to be more than just stress. She needed a triple bypass. It wasn't the fact that she was only 36 years old that put her in the record books at St. Vincent's Hospital. It was that she was female—their first. My younger sister and I were only 12 and 15 years old respectively, but we stayed alone during those three weeks of her hospital stay. Needless to say, my rose-colored glasses were really put to the test.

That time defined my outlook on life and even on my career. I've always refused to give up and see my glass as half empty. I wrote in high school and became enamored with seeing my byline in the school paper. I majored in journalism and went on to write for advertising agencies. Then I moved on to a career in publishing. Prior to meeting my husband, I dated all the wrong men and bounced from job to job, state to state, never once feeling as if I were running from anything, only running toward the rest of my life.

Not too long ago, an editor challenged me to pitch a book idea on a subject in which I consider myself an expert. But suddenly I had a tough time deciding what in the world that could be. Am I an expert wife or an expert mother? Nah. An expert advertising writer? Certainly not. How about a person who has always had the ability to see the brighter side of life and remain downright giddy most of the time?

These days I'm a published author. Am I happy about it? Sure I am. But I'm even happier that my 67-years-young mother was able to read my dedication:

To the woman who bestowed a pet name on me as a little girl that shaped my outlook forever.

I love you so,

"Sunshine"

A sign of a good mother is that each of her children thinks they are the favorite.

The Carriage Ride

One Christmas when Ramona came home to visit her parents, she asked her mother, "Do you remember the Christmas that we saved money in the fall for the horse-drawn carriage ride?"

Her mother remembered it only too well. When Ramona, the eldest of her four children, was six years old, Christmas came at a lean time. Ramona's father had been laid off from his job in the small town where they lived and was temporarily living in a distant city where he had found work. If he worked through the holidays he could earn much needed overtime pay.

Her parents couldn't bear the thought of the family spending Christmas apart, so the plan was for Ramona's mother to drive with the four children to the city where her husband was working. The children were wild with anticipation, because not only was Santa Claus coming, but they would also get to see Daddy!

One day Ramona came home from school, excited to report that the year before her friend had visited the city where they would be spending Christmas, and that she had taken a horse-drawn carriage ride just like in *Cinderella.* "Could we take one, too? Please, Mama?" cried Ramona.

Ramona's mother knew it would be expensive, but she couldn't resist the sparkle in her daughter's eyes when she spoke. "Maybe," she answered carefully, "but if you really want to do that, you need to help me save."

When the family walked to church, Ramona hung a bag on the back of her little brother's stroller and collected soda cans to return for the deposit money. She helped her mother clip coupons out of the newspaper and watched as her mother redeemed them at the grocery store. And when Christmas finally came and she and her mother took the carriage ride around the beautifully decorated city streets in the snow, Ramona felt as if she were in a fairy tale.

Her mother, though, had always felt bad that times were hard when her daughter was young. She told the grown-up Ramona apologetically, "I'm sorry we had to scrimp so much when you were little."

"Are you kidding?" Ramona exclaimed. "That is one of my best memories."

"I remember you saying you felt like a princess in a fairy tale," her mother replied, feeling a little better.

"It wasn't just the ride," Ramona said. "It was saving for it, too. From that I learned about anticipation, about making goals and achieving them, about sacrifice, and about not spending money you don't have. But I also learned about a mother's love. And that's what I'll remember the most."

❧❧

A mother's gift is two-fold—she takes care of you when you are young and teaches you to take care of yourself when you are older.

Never Give Up

I woke up in the hospital emergency room cursing in front of my mother. Even now I cringe with fear of being grounded for using bad language, and I'm a grown woman.

I had been in an accident and had a fractured skull and various other injuries. Under the circumstances, my mother ignored my cursing, and I could see that her face was white with the shock of seeing her child in so much pain. Looking back, I sort of wonder if it wasn't my colorful language.

In the days that followed, I was in more pain than I have ever known. Even after giving birth four times, the pain of my injuries was incomparable. So many times I felt as though I couldn't take any more. Yet every time I wanted to give up, my sweet mother appeared. Every time I awoke, she was sitting quietly at my bedside. And when she could see my frustration, my agony, she would distract me by talking about my sisters,

about our neighbors, and about my friends who were so supportive. She talked about my future, when I would become a grandmother, patiently reminding me of how much I had to look forward to. She quietly forced me not to give up.

She showed me that there is always good to counter the bad. She made me laugh and made me smile. And little by little, I grew stronger, both physically and emotionally. I felt like I was slowly seeing the storm come to an end and the sun peeking out behind the clouds.

All these years later, I have been through my share of trauma with my own children, and I have had plenty of bumps along the road of life. Whenever things feel overwhelming, I think of my sweet, patient mother. I remember the way she single-handedly taught me to look for the good within the bad. She showed me that there is always light and hope in the world, and no matter how bad things seem they will always get better. And to never, ever give up.

The Memory Box

Having been settled into our new home for almost a year, I decided to finish unpacking those last few boxes. Hidden low in the stack was a box simply marked "Jacob." Excitement jolted my empty-nest heart upon seeing the name of my eldest son, who was living 1,000 miles away.

Delighted, I spent hours pouring through the artwork, awards, and report cards that brought me right back to his childhood.

I found Jacob's soccer trading card at age six and a Mother's Day card from when he was nine that included coupons for extra chores, neck rubs, and breakfast in bed. I found an award Jacob won in the second grade for top sales in a school fundraiser. He'd gotten first place in the entire elementary school. Even at the age of seven, he had a way with people.

Tucked inside the "Jacob" box was a little baggie holding a tiny baby tooth. "Jacob's first tooth," was written in marker on the bag, and a folded piece of loose-leaf paper was stapled to the bag. I carefully removed the paper and read the note in his awkward, just-learning-how-to-write print.

Dear Tooth Fairy,

I love you. Please leave me a lot of money.

Love from your best friend, Jacob.

P.S. Don't keep my tooth.

I laughed until I cried. How I missed my little guy.

Now 25, Jacob had his own life and a serious girlfriend. I knew it wouldn't be long before he had children of his own. I pictured him with a little one on his knee, helping her write her first letter to the Tooth Fairy.

Each page in a book from his school years had a small school photo for that grade glued to it. If I flipped the pages fast, I could see the transformation from preschool to his senior year in high school. It was like watching him morph into an adult right before my eyes.

This unexpected trip down memory lane was the best way I could think of to spend my Saturday. This is one box I will never unpack and put away. It's one to keep close by, and on days when my heart longs for my firstborn, I will dig it out, open a box of tissues, and let the memories come home again.

Mother's Day with Marigolds

Easter in India, far from my children and grandchildren, was poignant. My new friends kept me busy from Good Friday through Easter Sunday with a Hindu wedding, parties, and sunrise service at the only church in the predominantly Hindu village. I had volunteered to work with a charity staffed by Indians for six months, and I was willing to give up a family Easter for the greater good of helping those living in the slum improve their lives.

Their children called me "auntie." I had an Easter egg hunt for them, which required boiling eggs over my one-burner gas stove and dying them with local products. Their finds were more than colored eggs: They were the only lunch these children could expect to have. In the slum, two meals a day are unusual; most people get by with only one.

As Mother's Day approached, I shared the tradition with the Indian women I worked with. I did not tell them that my heart was growing sick because my Mother's Day celebration would consist of only e-mails. I began counting the days until I could go home.

Mother's Day began with Sunday service, then my coworkers gave the rickshaw driver strange directions. Instead of going to my hotel room, we headed to the slum. There, the women giggled so much that they were covering their mouths with their saris.

They translated the huge banner at the slum's entrance: "Happy Mother's Day, Auntie!" More than a hundred people welcomed me to their community of thatched huts. Each child held one marigold, and I gathered them with hugs and smiles. One mother braided them along with other fragrant flowers, creating a beautiful lei.

They offered me a chair they had decorated like a throne and served me a meal of white rice and meat on a banana leaf. The children sang a song they had written in Hindi. A colleague leaned in and whispered that in their language, the words rhymed. The song greeted their auntie from the United States, who today became a mother they love.

Back in my room, my sweet-smelling lei around my neck, I read e-mails from my family back home. When I wrote back, it took me five paragraphs to describe all the love I had received from these wonderful people whose language I didn't even know. After I hit the send button, my weeks remaining in India felt just about right.

Growing Down

My five-year-old daughter, Alissa, had two favorite things: her best friend Kailyn and my red silk dress. As a single mother, I had only one elegant dress. I wore it on special occasions when dancing would be part of the evening's events. It cost too much, but like my sister says, "Sometimes a woman, even a mom, just has to put on a red dress and dance."

Alissa adored my red dress. She did not understand why she couldn't play dress up in it. While I let her and Kailyn play "Going to Church" in my skirts and blouses, "Going to the Gym" in my workout clothes, and "Going to the Market" while tripping over my jeans, I would not let them play "Going Dancing" in anything more exciting than my nightgowns.

Alissa was a well-behaved child, but she had already endured time-outs for putting on my red dress twice: once while I was mowing the lawn and another time while I was on a phone call that she had expected to last longer. One day I realized the girls were missing. My search ended in my closet, where Kailyn and Alissa were looking scared and holding hands. "We just wanted to touch it," Alissa said in such a wistful voice I did not have the heart to punish her.

After Kailyn left, I sat Alissa down with a cookie. I finally had the answer, and I felt like mother of the year. "Sweetie, I know how much you love your blue velvet dress." Her eyes sparkled at the mention of it. "You were careful when you wore it to your kindergarten concert. And at your grandmother's birthday dinner, you used your napkin and did not get a single crumb on your dress." This made her smile proudly. I continued, "If Kailyn asked to borrow your blue dress, what would you say?"

"I would tell her to use her napkin," she said in a breezy, matter-of-fact way.

My mother-of-the-year award evaporated.

The next time I pulled on my red silk dress to go dancing, I let Alissa zip it up and felt her little hand linger on the fabric. "I promise," I blurted out, "that I'm saving this dress for you when you grow up."

She hugged me tightly, but at this moment, she was the one with the surprise. "And I'll save my blue dress for you," she said, "for when you grow down."

Shake It Up

Anne was already waiting for her older sister, Ro, at their mom Mary's house. Mary had been divorced for four years, and the two sisters had decided they'd had enough of her loneliness and insistence that life ended the day their dad walked out and married his assistant.

"We have a surprise for you," Ro announced. She and Anne grabbed Mary's purse and jacket and literally pushed her out the front door, down the walk, and into Ro's SUV. A half hour later they pulled up to a dance studio, and Mary sighed.

"What are you girls trying to get me into now?" she asked, clearly as amused as she was anxious. The two girls said nothing, just opened the door for their mom, and helped her out.

The dance studio was bustling as the three women went into a back room where a dozen women stood waiting. Some wore shorts and tiny

tops, others had on lavish skirts and bra sets. Mary gasped, realizing what they were about to do.

The instructor came in and began wiggling her toned tummy to the enchanting Middle Eastern music, and Anne and Ro egged Mary to join in. Mary shook her head, embarrassed, but she noticed many of the women in the room were as old as she was. In fact, two were in their 70s. So she bit her lip and rolled up her T-shirt to reveal her less-than-perfect abs, then took a deep breath and let her stomach get into the belly-dancing groove.

Afterward, Anne and Ro watched with amusement and happiness as Mary went up to the instructor to register for a permanent spot in the class. When she came over to her daughters, she had a huge grin on her face.

"Wow, I haven't felt that sexy since high school!" she gushed, hugging her girls and thanking them for pushing her to try something new. As they left the studio, laughing and talking about what other new adventures they might try together, Anne and Ro watched as Mary shook her hips as she approached the car. Mary topped it off with a little tummy wiggle, and Ro and Anne eyeballed each other, wondering what they had gotten their mother into.

Cupcakes

When Jennifer found out she was pregnant with her first child, she felt the usual anxiety of a future mother—Would she be a good mom? Would she know what to do? Jennifer thought back to her own childhood, remembering how her mom, Sandra, always had the time and patience to deal with four active children.

"A mother's job is to give until it hurts," Sandra would lovingly tell her daughter. But she would always follow that with "and it hurts in a way that is so wonderful." Jennifer hoped she would soon find out exactly what her mom meant. She smiled, remembering a particular time when her mom truly went above and beyond the call of maternal duty. Jennifer had come home from school on a Thursday, anxious and worried. Her mom asked what was wrong, and Jennifer quietly replied that she had forgotten about a school party the next morning.

Her mom told her not to worry and said they would find her a pretty dress to wear. But it wasn't clothing Jennifer was worried about. It was the six dozen cupcakes she had promised her teacher that her mom would bake. When Sandra finally got the information out of her daughter, she was a bit stunned. Six dozen cupcakes? By morning? And with *no* ingredients in the house? But instead of yelling or sending Jennifer to her room without her supper, Sandra just smiled and said, "Oh, well. Then we're off to the store!"

Sandra quickly gathered up the kids and went to the local A&P to get all the supplies. Back at home she enlisted all four children to help in a bake-a-thon that lasted well into the night. Finally, they finished six dozen treats, and then Sandra bathed four tired and flour-haired children and put them to bed before tending to her own shower and rest.

The next morning Sandra drove Jennifer to school with six dozen cupcakes loaded into the trunk. Her teacher responded with a happy smile, never knowing about the chaos of the night before.

Jennifer put her hand on her stomach, wondering if it would be a boy or a girl. She wondered how joyful it would be when she, too, experienced that love so strong it hurts—and hurts wonderfully.

Always By My Side

The news struck Jane like a direct blow to the stomach. Her New York–based company had just announced that half their sales force would be relocating to Japan. Jane was the sales director. Within two weeks she was expected to uproot her life and move to a foreign country where she barely knew the language or the culture. Her boss explained that learning Japanese would be easy once the team was settled, but Jane was anxious and depressed, especially about leaving her aging mother, Lil.

When she broke the news to Lil, Jane waited for the other shoe to drop. Her mom had supported her in every step of her career and never questioned her decisions, but Jane knew part of the reason was because as sales director, she didn't have to travel—she delegated that to her sales force while she held a comfortable desk job. Now she would indeed be traveling, permanently, to another country. Lil just smiled proudly

when Jane broke the news, surprising Jane, who was sure her mom would become downright upset, begging her daughter not to leave.

But Lil stayed quiet and supportive throughout the next two weeks, offering advice and courage as Jane packed and planned and worried and fretted. Often, Lil would calm her daughter by saying, "It will all work out for the best," which seemed to be her personal motto.

Jane's first week in Japan was exciting, but it was nerve-racking getting to know her way around. Jane missed her mom and felt guilty about leaving her behind in the States, with only distant relatives to look after her. One night Jane was in tears, having gotten lost in a town where no one spoke English. She had just found her way home when her text-message tone went off. Jane checked her text messages. There was one from Lil that simply said, "It will all work out for the best."

Jane smiled and picked up the phone, not caring what time it was in New York. Lil answered on the first ring, and Jane didn't even say hello before she burst out, "How would you like to come live in Japan with me?" Lil responded immediately, "I've always loved sushi!" Jane and Lil then spent the next 15 minutes making long-distance plans to close the distance between them.

The Magic Recipe

After my marriage fell apart, my teenage son, Jack, took the news of the divorce really hard. Our children were very close, and my five-year-old daughter desperately wanted to make it all better for her big brother.

Maya got her writing gene from her mother and decided that writing her brother a note would be the best medicine. She wanted to write it in a card and had just enough money for one of those little cards you attach to a present. It had a picture of a puppy and a kitten on the front, and she was pleased with her choice, thinking it reminded her of her and Jack.

I watched as she sat, feet tucked under her, thinking hard about just the right thing to say. She wrote carefully in her five-year-old print, then looked up and asked me a question.

"Mommy, how do you spell 'forever'?"

My heart did a happy dance, and I knew that somehow she was going to make her big brother smile. I helped her spell the magic word, and my heart glowed.

Maya found Jack's skateboard outside of his best friend's house, tucked her little card under the peeling deck of his board, and left it for him to find. Jack came home for dinner, walked in the kitchen with a huge grin, and came right over to his little sister. Giving her a big hug, he said a simple "Thanks," and I sensed things were going to be all right with him. We sat down to dinner together, and our home was once again filled with the happy chatter of a family together.

That night as I said good night to Jack, he showed me Maya's little card. I opened it and read the note inside.

Jack I love you. Forever. Love, Maya

My daughter's simple gesture of love for her big brother was the magic recipe that reminded me that even though the shape of it may have changed, one thing would never change. Our family is forever.

I Was Just Thinking About You!

It was uncanny sometimes how strong the bond was between Julie and her mother. It was so strong that sometimes it was difficult for Julie to break away. In fact, the first summer she went to camp as a little girl, she didn't call home the first few days, even though she had the opportunity. She was having a wonderful time, but she was afraid that at the sound of her mother's voice she would get homesick and burst into tears. Midway through camp, though, she knew she was going to make it. When she swam well enough to get a lifesaver's badge and survived a bout of poison ivy, she decided to call her mom to give her the news. She was a little afraid that her mother's feelings would be hurt that she hadn't called sooner. But she knew it would be okay when her mother heard her voice and said cheerfully, "Sweetheart! I was just thinking about you!"

The same thing happened when she went to college. Wanting to establish her independence, Julie waited until she had gotten to know her roommate, learned her way around campus, and passed her first pop quiz with flying colors to call her mom, who answered immediately, "Honey! I was just thinking about you!"

When Julie found out that she was expecting her first child, she called her mother right away and got the greeting she had come to expect. After her daughter, Sarah, was born, Julie was sometimes frustrated with Sarah's stubbornness. Julie's mother would smile knowingly, seeing how her granddaughter exhibited the same streak of independence that Julie always had. The first time Sarah went away from home, it was to stay with her cousins for a week. Julie worried that her daughter would be homesick and waited anxiously for a call that didn't come for several days. As soon as she heard Sarah say hesitantly, "Mom?" she found herself answering, "Honey! I was just thinking about you!"

Raising children, mothers learn to raise their voices just one notch above the noise.

The Swimming Lesson

Boy, did I want to swim. A water lover by nature, it was hard not to dive in and let the cool water surround me. Being in the water makes me happy and relaxed, but embarrassment about my postpartum body kept me from doing the thing I loved most.

"C'mon, Mom! Get in!" my kids hollered at me.

The blue-green water beckoned me. I thought back to the days when putting on a swimsuit was nothing more than putting on a swimsuit. I had spent hours playing water volleyball, laughing and feeling completely carefree. I closed my eyes and could almost feel the water carry me away, freeing me from everyday life and surrounding me with good, old-fashioned fun.

"Mommy, Mommy!" my kids chanted. By now I was thoroughly mortified that everyone in the pool area knew I was too embarrassed to go swimming. I could see them whispering to each other. Grinning, my little ones climbed out of the pool.

"We're not swimming until you get in." They were using the guilt tactic—a bargaining device that is usually my tool. I could see that they were serious, and then I realized that if they weren't embarrassed about me wearing a swimsuit in public, why should I be? I knew I would regret it if I missed out, and I was tired of regretting things. I wanted to be glad that I did something for once, not sorry that I didn't.

Hopping up, I headed for our room and changed into my suit as quickly as I could before I changed my mind. With my beach towel wrapped around my hips, I scurried down to the pool. As I walked into the poolroom, I flung the towel off and dove in without a second's hesitation. When I came up for air, my family was grinning and shouting, "Go Mom!" We played for a long, long time, and I loved it.

"Mommy, you look so pretty when you're laughing," my daughter said as we were climbing out of the pool. I suddenly realized what great teachers my kids are.

I haven't had a swimming lesson since I was eight years old, but this lesson from my children taught me that if they can unconditionally love me, then I owe it to them to love myself the same way.

Contributing Writers

Rebecca Christian is a Des Moines–based writer, poet, and playwright who can be reached at rebecca.christian@mchsi.com.

Lain Ehmann is a California–based writer and mom to three.

Susan Farr Fahncke is founder of the inspirational Web site, www.2TheHeart.com. She can be contacted at susan@2theheart.com.

Marie D. Jones is author of several nonfiction books and coauthor of more than three dozen inspirational books. She is an ordained minister.

Julie Clark Robinson is the award-winning author of *Live in the Moment.* You can learn more about her at www.julieclarkrobinson.com.

Carol Stigger is a writer specializing in microcredit and poverty in developing countries. She works with a microcredit organization in India during the winter and lives in Italy every spring, writing travel articles and fiction.

Cover illustrations: Tina Dorman

Illustrators: Lynda Calvert-Weyant, Tina Dorman, Alyssa Hemsath-Mooney, Paula McArdle